MW00512587

NO GALLBLADDER DIET

MEGA BUNDLE – 3 Manuscripts in 1 – 120+ No Gallbladder - friendly recipes including pizza, side dishes, and casseroles for a delicious and tasty diet

TABLE OF CONTENTS

3

Introduction

No Gallbladder recipes for personal enjoyment but also for family enjoyment. You will love them for sure for how easy it is to prepare them.

ROAST RECIPES

ROASTED SQUASH

Serves: *3-4*

Prep Time: *10*   Minutes

Cook Time: *20*   Minutes

Total Time: *30*   Minutes

INGREDIENTS

- 2 delicata squashes
- 2 tablespoons olive oil
- 1 tsp curry powder
- 1 tsp salt

DIRECTIONS

1. Preheat the oven to 400 F
2. Cut everything in half lengthwise
3. Toss everything with olive oil and place onto a prepared baking sheet
4. Roast for 18-20 minutes at 400 F or until golden brown
5. When ready remove from the oven and serve

ROASTED CARROT

Serves: **3-4**

Prep Time: **10**   Minutes

Cook Time: **20**   Minutes

Total Time: **30**   Minutes

INGREDIENTS

- 1 lb. carrot
- 2 tablespoons olive oil
- 1 tsp curry powder
- 1 tsp salt

DIRECTIONS

1. Preheat the oven to 400 F
2. Cut everything in half lengthwise
3. Toss everything with olive oil and place onto a prepared baking sheet
4. Roast for 18-20 minutes at 400 F or until golden brown
5. When ready remove from the oven and serve

ZUCCHINI SOUP

Serves: **4**

Prep Time: **10** Minutes

Cook Time: **20** Minutes

Total Time: **30** Minutes

INGREDIENTS

- 1 tablespoon olive oil
- 1 lb. zucchini
- ¼ red onion
- ½ cup all-purpose flour
- ¼ tsp salt
- ¼ tsp pepper
- 1 can vegetable broth
- 1 cup heavy cream

DIRECTIONS

1. In a saucepan heat olive oil and sauté zucchini until tender
2. Add remaining ingredients to the saucepan and bring to a boil
3. When all the vegetables are tender transfer to a blender and blend until smooth
4. Pour soup into bowls, garnish with parsley and serve

CHICKEN NUGGETS

Serves: *3*

Prep Time: *10*   Minutes

Cook Time: *25*   Minutes

Total Time: *35*   Minutes

INGREDIENTS

- 2 chicken breasts
- ¼ cup almond flour
- 1 tablespoon seasoning
- 1 tablespoon olive oil
- ½ tsp salt
- ¼ tsp pepper

DIRECTIONS

1. Preheat the oven to 375 F
2. In a bowl add seasoning, salt, almond flour, pepper
3. Add pieces of chicken breast into your bowl and cover with flour
4. Transfer to your baking sheet
5. Bake 18-20 minutes, remove and serve

BEEF FAJITAS

Serves: **3**

Prep Time: **10**   Minutes

Cook Time: **20**   Minutes

Total Time: **30**   Minutes

INGREDIENTS

- 1 lb. beef stir-fry strips
- 1 red onion
- 1 red bell pepper
- ¼ tsp tsp cumin
- ¼ tsp chili powder
- salt
- pepper
- 1 avocado

DIRECTIONS

1. In a skillet add strips and stir-fry, add salt, pepper and cook for 2-3 minute and set aside
2. Add onions, bell peppers, chili powder, cumin and fry for 2-3 minutes
3. Remove to a plate and serve with avocado

SUMMER SALMON

Serves: **4**
Prep Time: **10**   Minutes

Cook Time: **30**   Minutes

Total Time: **40**   Minutes

INGREDIENTS

- 3 salmon fillets
- 2 leeks
- 6 oz. asparagus spears
- 1 cup sugar snap peas
- 3 tablespoons white wine
- 1 cup vegetable broth
- 1 tablespoon chives
- salt

DIRECTIONS

1. In a Dutch oven add salmon, asparagus, wine, peas, chicken bean and pepper
2. Bring to boil and simmer for 12-15 minutes
3. Sprinkle with chives and serve

GRILLED SALMON

Serves: **4**

Prep Time: **10** Minutes

Cook Time: **20** Minutes

Total Time: **30** Minutes

INGREDIENTS

- Juice of 1 lime
- 2 tablespoons basil
- 3 salmon fillets
- 2 tablespoons salmon fillets
- 2 cup low-fat yogurt
- 1 tablespoon mayonnaise
- ½ tsp lime zest
- salt
- mixed salad leaves

DIRECTIONS

1. In a bowl mix pepper, basil, lime juice, salt and pepper
2. Add salmon fillets and let it marinade for 20-30 minutes
3. In another bowl mix lime zest, basil, mayonnaise, yogurt and salt
4. Preheat the oven to 400 F and place the salmon fillets on a ridged grill pan

5. Brush the salmon with marinade and grill for 4-5 minutes per side
6. When ready remove and serve

Serves: **12**

Prep Time: **10** Minutes

Cook Time: **20** Minutes

Total Time: **30** Minutes

INGREDIENTS

- 1 lemon
- juice 1 lime
- 1 tablespoon olive oil
- 1 tsp honey
- 1 garlic clove
- 1 tablespoon oregano
- 1 tablespoon parsley
- 6 oz. monkfish fillet
- 12 fresh mussels
- 1 yellow bell pepper
- 1 zucchini
- 12 cherry tomatoes
- salt

DIRECTIONS

1. In a bowl add lime juice, honey, lemon zest, garlic, oregano and salt and mix well, marinade for 50-60 minutes

2. Prepare 10-12 wooden skewers and add on each one skewer 1 cube of monkfish, 1 piece of bell pepper, 1 zucchini, 1 mussel and a cherry tomato

3. Grill each kebab for 10-12 minutes or until done

4. When ready, remove and serve

POTATO TORTILLA

Serves: **6**

Prep Time: **10**   Minutes

Cook Time: **20**   Minutes

Total Time: **30**   Minutes

INGREDIENTS

- 1,5 lb. potatoes
- 1 tablespoon olive oil
- 1 red onion
- 1 zucchini
- 1 slice turkey bacon
- 5 eggs
- 1 tablespoon parsley
- pepper

DIRECTIONS

1. In a saucepan add potato cubes, water and bring to a boil
2. In a skillet add potatoes, bacon, zucchini and cook until potatoes are tender
3. In a bowl beat the eggs, add water, pepper, parsley, pour the egg mixture over the vegetables and cook for 4-5 minutes
4. Slide the tortilla onto a plate, cool for 2-3 minutes and cut into wedges and serve

Serves: **2**
Prep Time: **10**   Minutes

Cook Time: **10**   Minutes

Total Time: **20**   Minutes

INGREDIENTS

-   ½ lb. dried noodles
-   1 lb. Asian stir-fry vegetables
-   ½ cups hoisin sauce
-   1 tsp chili flakes

DIRECTIONS

1. In a frying pan add vegetables, water and stir-fry for 4-5 minutes
2. Add hoisin sauce, noodles, chili flakes and toss to coat, remove and serve

APRICOT CHICKEN PATTIES

Serves: **4**

Prep Time: **10** Minutes

Cook Time: **10** Minutes

Total Time: **20** Minutes

INGREDIENTS

- 1 lb. chicken mince
- 2 slices bread
- 3 oz. pistachio nuts
- 1/3 lb. dried apricots

DIRECTIONS

1. In a bowl mix combine the mince, apricots, bread, pistachios and season with pepper
2. Roll into o4 patties and cook for 4-5 minutes per side
3. Remove and serve

GREEN PESTO PASTA

Serves: **2**
Prep Time: **5**   Minutes

Cook Time: **15**   Minutes

Total Time: **20**   Minutes

INGREDIENTS

- 4 oz. spaghetti
- 2 cups basil leaves
- 2 garlic cloves
- ¼ cup olive oil
- 2 tablespoons parmesan cheese
- ½ tsp black pepper

DIRECTIONS

1. Bring water to a boil and add pasta
2. In a blend add parmesan cheese, basil leaves, garlic and blend
3. Add olive oil, pepper and blend again
4. Pour pesto onto pasta and serve when ready

Serves: **2**

Prep Time: **10** Minutes

Cook Time: **10** Minutes

Total Time: **20** Minutes

INGREDIENTS

- 3 Atlantic salmon fillets
- 2 tsp olive oil
- 1 clove garlic
- 1 tablespoon rosemary
- black pepper
- 1 tablespoon lemon juice
- 1 tablespoon white wine

DIRECTIONS

1. In a frying pan sauté garlic, rosemary and pepper for 1-2 minutes
2. Add fish and cook for 1-2 minutes per side

MUSHROOM BURGERS

Serves: *2*
Prep Time: *10*   Minutes

Cook Time: *10*   Minutes

Total Time: *20*   Minutes

INGREDIENTS

- 2 tablespoons olive oil
- 1 lb. mushrooms
- 1 lb. beef mince
- 1 onion
- 1 tsp Worcestershire sauce
- 1 egg
- 4 hamburger buns
- 1 cup lettuce
- 4 slices tomatoes
- salt

DIRECTIONS

1. In a frying pan add mushrooms and cook for 4-5 minutes, remove and set aside
2. In a bowl mix beef mince, salt, pepper, Worcestershire sauce, mushrooms, onion and mix well
3. Form into 2 patties, and refrigerate for 10-15 minutes

4. In a frying pan cook patty for 2-3 minutes per side and also grill hamburger buns

5. Top buns with lettuce, tomatoes and patties

6. Serve when ready

BLACK BEANS BURGERS

Serves: **4**

Prep Time: **10**   Minutes

Cook Time: **20**   Minutes

Total Time: **30**   Minutes

INGREDIENTS

- 1 lb. black beans
- 1 cup brown rice
- 1 onion
- 1 onion
- ¼ tsp tabasco sauce
- 1 egg
- ½ cup bread crumbs
- 5 tablespoons salsa
- 4 hamburger buns
- ½ cups yoghurt
- 4 leaves romaine lettuce
- 1 avocado

DIRECTIONS

1. Preheat the oven to 325 F
2. In a bowl mix mashed beans, onions, tabasco sauce, rice, egg, breadcrumbs and mix well

3. Divide mixture into patties and bake for 12-15 minutes or until done
4. In another bowl mix yoghurt and salsa, serve with lettuce and avocado

CABBAGE FRITATTA

Serves: **2**

Prep Time: **10** Minutes

Cook Time: **20** Minutes

Total Time: **30** Minutes

INGREDIENTS

- ½ lb. cabbage
- 1 tablespoon olive oil
- ½ red onion
- 2 eggs
- ¼ tsp salt
- 2 oz. cheddar cheese
- 1 garlic clove
- ¼ tsp dill

DIRECTIONS

1. In a bowl whisk eggs with salt and cheese
2. In a frying pan heat olive oil and pour egg mixture
3. Add remaining ingredients and mix well
4. Serve when ready

BRUSSEL SPROUTS FRITATTA

Serves: *2*

Prep Time: *10*   Minutes

Cook Time: *20*   Minutes

Total Time: *30*   Minutes

INGREDIENTS

- ½ lb. Brussel sprouts
- 1 tablespoon olive oil
- ½ red onion
- ¼ tsp salt
- 2 eggs
- 2 oz. cheddar cheese
- 1 garlic clove
- ¼ tsp dill

DIRECTIONS

1. In a skillet sauté Brussel sprouts until tender
2. In a bowl whisk eggs with salt and cheese
3. In a frying pan heat olive oil and pour egg mixture
4. Add remaining ingredients and mix well
5. Serve when ready

CELERY FRITATTA

Serves: **2**

Prep Time: **10** Minutes

Cook Time: **20** Minutes

Total Time: **30** Minutes

INGREDIENTS

- 1 cup celery
- 1 tablespoon olive oil
- ½ red onion
- ¼ tsp salt
- 2 eggs
- 2 oz. cheddar cheese
- 1 garlic clove
- ¼ tsp dill

DIRECTIONS

1. In a bowl whisk eggs with salt and cheese
2. In a frying pan heat olive oil and pour egg mixture
3. Add remaining ingredients and mix well
4. When ready serve with sautéed celery

PROSCIUTTO FRITATTA

Serves: **2**

Prep Time: **10**   Minutes

Cook Time: **20**   Minutes

Total Time: **30**   Minutes

INGREDIENTS

- 8-10 slices prosciutto
- 1 tsp rosemary
- 1 tablespoon olive oil
- ½ red onion
- ¼ tsp salt
- 2 eggs
- 2 oz. parmesan cheese
- 1 garlic clove
- ¼ tsp dill

DIRECTIONS

1. In a bowl whisk eggs with salt and parmesan cheese
2. In a frying pan heat olive oil and pour egg mixture
3. Add remaining ingredients and mix well
4. When prosciutto and eggs are cooked remove from heat and serve

Serves: **2**

Prep Time: **10**   Minutes

Cook Time: **20**   Minutes

Total Time: **30**   Minutes

INGREDIENTS

- 1 tsp oregano
- 1 tablespoon olive oil
- ½ red onion
- ¼ tsp salt
- 2 eggs
- 2 oz. cheddar cheese
- 1 garlic clove
- ¼ tsp dill

DIRECTIONS

1. In a bowl whisk eggs with salt and cheese
2. In a frying pan heat olive oil and pour egg mixture
3. Add remaining ingredients and mix well
4. Serve when ready

HUMMUS WRAP

Serves: *2*
Prep Time: *5*   Minutes

Cook Time: *5*   Minutes

Total Time: *10* Minutes

INGREDIENTS

- 1 cup cooked brown rice
- 1 gluten-free tortilla
- 2-3 tablespoons hummus
- ¼ cup black beans
- ¼ cup tomatoes
- ¼ cup cucumber
- ¼ cup avocado
- ¼ cup romaine lettuce

DIRECTIONS

1. Microwave the tortilla for 20-30 seconds
2. Spread hummus on tortilla
3. Add beans, tomatoes, cucumber, and remaining ingredients
4. Roll like a burrito and serve

POTATO WEDGES

Serves: **4-6**

Prep Time: **10**   Minutes

Cook Time: **30**   Minutes

Total Time: **40**   Minutes

INGREDIENTS

- 2 white potatoes
- 1 tsp olive oil
- 1 tsp garlic powder
- 1 tsp onion powder
- salt
- 1 cup avocado dip

DIRECTIONS

1. Slice potatoes into thick slices
2. In a bowl combine garlic powder, onion powder, salt, olive oil and mix well
3. Place the potatoes into the mixture and stir to coat
4. Bake the potatoes at 425 F for 25-30 minutes
5. When ready remove from the oven and serve with avocado dip

KALE CHIPS

Serves: **4**

Prep Time: **10** Minutes

Cook Time: **15** Minutes

Total Time: **25** Minutes

INGREDIENTS

- 2 cups kale
- 1 tablespoon avocado oil
- 1 tsp salt
- 1 tsp turmeric
- 1 tsp chili powder
- 1 tsp curry powder

DIRECTIONS

1. In a bowl combine all ingredients except kale
2. Mix well and add kale to the seasoning mixture
3. Toss to coat and then place the kale in a baking dish
4. Bake at 250 F for 12-15 minutes
5. When ready remove from the oven and serve

EGG ROLL BOWL

Serves: **2**

Prep Time: **10**   Minutes

Cook Time: **20**   Minutes

Total Time: **30**   Minutes

INGREDIENTS

- 1 tablespoon olive oil
- 1 clove garlic
- 1 lb. pork
- ½ red onion
- 1 cup carrot
- 1 cabbage
- ½ cup soy sauce
- ¼ tsp black pepper

DIRECTIONS

1. In a skillet sauté garlic and onion until soft
2. Add pork, cabbage and cook for another 6-7 minutes
3. Add soy sauce, carrot and cook until vegetables are tender
4. When ready transfer mixture to a bowl, add pepper and serve

Serves: **1**

Prep Time: **10** Minutes

Cook Time: **20** Minutes

Total Time: **30** Minutes

INGREDIENTS

- 1 tablespoon olive oil
- 1 chicken breast
- 1 tsp oregano
- 1 tsp black pepper
- 1 cup tomatoes
- ¼ cucumber
- ¼ cup red onion
- ¼ cup black olives
- 1/4 cup feta cheese
- 1 cup dressing

DIRECTIONS

1. In a skillet add chicken and cook until golden
2. Add seasoning and onion
3. When ready place all ingredients in a bowl
4. Drizzle dressing on top, mix well and serve

CRANBERRY SALAD

Serves: **2**

Prep Time: **5**   Minutes

Cook Time: **15** Minutes

Total Time: **20** Minutes

INGREDIENTS

- ½ cup celery
- 1 packet Knox Gelatin
- 1 cup cranberry juice
- 1 can berry cranberry sauce
- 1 cup sour cream

DIRECTIONS

1. In a pan add juice, gelatin, cranberry sauce and cook on low heat
2. Add sour cream, celery and continue to cook
3. Pour mixture into a pan
4. Serve when ready

GAZPACHO SALAD

Serves: **4**

Prep Time: **10** Minutes

Cook Time: **30** Minutes

Total Time: **40** Minutes

INGREDIENTS

- ½ lb. cherry tomatoes
- ½ cucumber
- 3 oz. cooked quinoa
- 1 tsp bouillon powder
- 2 spring onions
- 1 red pepper
- ½ avocado
- 1 pack Japanese tofu

DIRECTIONS

1. In a bowl combine all ingredients together
2. Add salad dressing, toss well and serve

Serves: *4*
Prep Time: *10*   Minutes

Cook Time: *30*   Minutes

Total Time: *40*   Minutes

INGREDIENTS

- 1 tsp olive oil
- ¼ lb. tomatoes
- 2 oz. radish
- 1 oz. parsley
- 1 tablespoon coriander
- salt

DIRECTIONS

1. In a bowl combine all ingredients together and mix well
2. Add salad dressing, toss well and serve

ZUCCHINI & BELL PEPPER SALAD

Serves: *1*

Prep Time: *5*   Minutes

Cook Time: *5*   Minutes

Total Time: *10*   Minutes

INGREDIENTS

- ¼ cup zucchini
- ¼ cup red capsicum
- ½ cup yellow capsicum
- 1 cup sprouted moong
- ¼ cup apple
- 1 tablespoon olive oil
- 1 tsp lemon juice

DIRECTIONS

1. In a bowl combine all ingredients together and mix well
2. Add olive oil, toss well and serve

QUINOA & AVOCADO SALAD

Serves:	*1*
Prep Time:	*5* Minutes
Cook Time:	*5* Minutes
Total Time:	*10* Minutes

INGREDIENTS

- ¼ cooked quinoa
- ¼ cup avocado
- ¼ cup zucchini
- ¼ cup capsicum cubes
- ¼ cup mushroom
- ½ cup cherry tomatoes
- 1 cup lettuce
- 1 tablespoon sprouts
- 1 tsp olive oil
- Salad dressing

DIRECTIONS

1. In a bowl combine all ingredients together and mix well
2. Add salad dressing, toss well and serve

TOFU SALAD

Serves: **1**

Prep Time: **5** Minutes

Cook Time: **5** Minutes

Total Time: **10** Minutes

INGREDIENTS

- 1 pack tofu
- 1 cup chopped vegetables (carrots, cucumber)

DRESSING

- 1 tablespoon sesame oil
- 1 tablespoon mustard
- 1 tablespoon brown rice vinegar
- 1 tablespoon soya sauce

DIRECTIONS

1. In a bowl combine all ingredients together and mix well
2. Add salad dressing, toss well and serve

PAD THAI SALAD

Serves: *1*

Prep Time: *5* Minutes

Cook Time: *5* Minutes

Total Time: *10* Minutes

INGREDIENTS

- ¼ lb. rice noodles
- 1 red pepper
- 1 onion
- 4 stalks coriander
- ¼ package silken tofu
- 1 oz. roasted peanuts
- Salad dressing

DIRECTIONS

1. In a bowl combine all ingredients together and mix well
2. Add salad dressing, toss well and serve

AVOCADO SALAD

Serves: *1*

Prep Time: *5*   Minutes

Cook Time: *5*   Minutes

Total Time: *10*   Minutes

INGREDIENTS

- 2 avocados
- ¼ lb. snap peas
- 1 tablespoon sesame seeds

SALAD DRESSING

- 1 tablespoon soya sauce
- 1 tablespoon umeboshi puree
- 2 tablespoons mikawa mirin

DIRECTIONS

1. In a bowl combine all ingredients together and mix well
2. Add salad dressing, toss well and serve

MUSHROOM SALAD

Serves: *1*

Prep Time: *5*   Minutes

Cook Time: *5*   Minutes

Total Time: *10*   Minutes

INGREDIENTS

- ½ lb. mushrooms
- 1 clove garlic
- ½ lb. salad leaves
- ¼ lb. tofu
- 1 oz. walnuts
- salad dressing

DIRECTIONS

1. In a bowl combine all ingredients together and mix well
2. Add salad dressing, toss well and serve

MIXED GREENS SALAD

Serves: *1*
Prep Time: 5   Minutes

Cook Time: 5   Minutes

Total Time: *10*   Minutes

INGREDIENTS

- 2 cucumbers
- 3 radishes
- ¼ red bell pepper
- 2 spring onions
- 1 tablespoon red wine vinegar
- 1 tablespoon rice vinegar
- 1 tablespoon soya sauce
- 1 tablespoon clearspring mirin
- 2 cups mixed salad greens

DIRECTIONS

1. In a bowl combine all ingredients together and mix well
2. Add salad dressing, toss well and serve

Serves: **1**

Prep Time: **5** Minutes

Cook Time: **5** Minutes

Total Time: **10** Minutes

INGREDIENTS

- 1 cup cooked quinoa
- ¼ cup clearspring hijiki
- ¼ red bell pepper
- 1 bun watercress
- 2 radishes
- 2 tablespoons goji berries

DIRECTIONS

1. In a bowl combine all ingredients together and mix well
2. Add salad dressing, toss well and serve

FISH STEW

Serves: **4**

Prep Time: **15**   Minutes

Cook Time: **45**   Minutes

Total Time: **60**   Minutes

INGREDIENTS

- 1 fennel bulb
- 1 red onion
- 2 garlic cloves
- 2 tablespoons olive oil
- 1 cup white wine
- 1 tablespoon fennel seeds
- 4 bay leaves
- 2 cups chicken stock
- 8 oz. halibut
- 12 oz. haddock

DIRECTIONS

1. Chop all ingredients in big chunks
2. In a large pot heat olive oil and add ingredients one by one
3. Cook for 5-6 or until slightly brown

4. Add remaining ingredients and cook until tender, 35-45 minutes
5. Season while stirring on low heat
6. When ready remove from heat and serve

BUTTERNUT SQUASH STEW

Serves: **4**

Prep Time: **15**   Minutes

Cook Time: **45**   Minutes

Total Time: **60**   Minutes

INGREDIENTS

- 2 tablespoons olive oil
- 2 red onions
- 2 cloves garlic
- 1. Tablespoon rosemary
- 1 tablespoon thyme
- 2 lb. beef
- 1 cup white wine
- 1 cup butternut squash
- 2 cups beef broth
- ½ cup tomatoes
-

DIRECTIONS

1. Chop all ingredients in big chunks
2. In a large pot heat olive oil and add ingredients one by one
3. Cook for 5-6 or until slightly brown
4. Add remaining ingredients and cook until tender, 35-45 minutes

5. Season while stirring on low heat
6. When ready remove from heat and serve

CASSEROLE RECIPES

BACON CASSEROLE

Serves: **4**

Prep Time: **10**   Minutes

Cook Time: **15**   Minutes

Total Time: **25**   Minutes

INGREDIENTS

- 4-5 slices bacon
- 3-4 tablespoons butter
- 5-6 tablespoons flour
- 2 cups milk
- 3 cups cheddar cheese
- 2 cups chicken breast
- 1 tsp seasoning mix

DIRECTIONS

1. Sauté the veggies and set aside
2. Preheat the oven to 425 F
3. Transfer the sautéed veggies to a baking dish, add remaining ingredients to the baking dish
4. Mix well, add seasoning and place the dish in the oven
5. Bake for 12-15 minutes or until slightly brown

6. When ready remove from the oven and serve

ENCHILADA CASSEROLE

Serves: **4**

Prep Time: **10**   Minutes

Cook Time: **25**   Minutes

Total Time: **35**   Minutes

INGREDIENTS

- 1 tablespoon olive oil
- 1 red onion
- 1 bell pepper
- 2 cloves garlic
- 1 can black beans
- 1 cup chicken
- 1 can green chilis
- 1 can enchilada sauce
- 1 cup cheddar cheese
- 1 cup sour cream

DIRECTIONS

1. Sauté the veggies and set aside
2. Preheat the oven to 425 F
3. Transfer the sautéed veggies to a baking dish, add remaining ingredients to the baking dish
4. Mix well, add seasoning and place the dish in the oven

5. Bake for 15-25 minutes or until slightly brown
6. When ready remove from the oven and serve

PIZZA RECIPES

CASSEROLE PIZZA

Serves: **6-8**
Prep Time: **10**   Minutes

Cook Time: **15**   Minutes

Total Time: **25**   Minutes

INGREDIENTS

- 1 pizza crust
- ½ cup tomato sauce
- ¼ black pepper
- 1 cup zucchini slices
- 1 cup mozzarella cheese
- 1 cup olives

DIRECTIONS

1. Spread tomato sauce on the pizza crust
2. Place all the toppings on the pizza crust
3. Bake the pizza at 425 F for 12-15 minutes
4. When ready remove pizza from the oven and serve

SECOND COOKBOOK

SIDE DISHES

FRIED VEGETABLES

Serves: *2*

Prep Time: *10*   Minutes

Cook Time: *15*   Minutes

Total Time: *25*   Minutes

INGREDIENTS

- 1 cup red bell pepper
- ¼ cup cucumber
- ¼ cup zucchini
- ¼ cup asparagus
- ¼ cup carrots
- 1 onion
- 2 eggs
- 1 tsp salt
- 1 tsp pepper
- Seasoning
- 1 tablespoon olive oil

DIRECTIONS

1. In a skillet heat olive oil and sauté onion until soft
2. Chop vegetables into thin slices and pour over onion

3. Whisk eggs with salt and pepper and pour over the vegetables

4. Cook until vegetables are brown

5. When ready remove from heat and serve

ONION SAUCE

Serves: **4**

Prep Time: **10** Minutes

Cook Time: **55** Minutes

Total Time: **65** Minutes

INGREDIENTS

- 1 onion
- 2 garlic cloves
- ¼ lb. carrots
- 1 potato
- 1 tablespoon balsamic vinegar
- ¼ tsp salt
- ¼ tsp black pepper
- 1 tablespoon olive oil
- 1 cup water

DIRECTIONS

1. Chop all the vegetables and place them in a heated skillet
2. Add remaining ingredients and cook on low heat
3. Allow to simmer for 40-45 minutes or until vegetables are soft
4. Transfer mixture to a blender and blend until smooth
5. When ready remove from the blender and serve

FISH "CAKE"

Serves: **4-6**

Prep Time: **10** Minutes

Cook Time: **50** Minutes

Total Time: **60** Minutes

INGREDIENTS

- 2 tuna tins
- 2 potatoes
- 2 eggs
- 1 handful of gluten free flour
- 1 handful of parsley
- black pepper
- 1 cup breadcrumbs

DIRECTIONS

1. Preheat the oven to 350 F
2. Boil the potatoes until they are soft
3. Mix the tuna with parsley, black pepper and salt
4. Roll fish into patties and dip into a bowl with flour, then eggs and then breadcrumbs
5. Place the patties on a baking tray
6. Bake at 350 F for 40-45 minutes
7. When ready remove from heat and serve

SUSHI HANDROLLS

Serves: *2*
Prep Time: *10* Minutes

Cook Time: *25* Minutes

Total Time: *35* Minutes

INGREDIENTS

- 1 sushi nori packet
- 4 tablespoons mayonnaise
- ½ lb. smoked salmon
- 1 tsp wasabi
- 1 cup cooked sushi rice
- 1 avocado

DIRECTIONS

1. Cut avocado and into thin slices
2. Take a sheet of sushi and spread mayonnaise onto the sheet
3. Add rice, salmon and avocado
4. Roll and dip sushi into wasabi and serve

STEAMED VEGETABLES

Serves: *2*
Prep Time: *10*   Minutes

Cook Time: *10*   Minutes

Total Time: *20*   Minutes

INGREDIENTS

- 1 carrot
- 2 sweet potato
- 2 parsnips
- 1 zucchini
- 2 broccoli stems

DIRECTIONS

1. Chop vegetables into thin slices
2. Place all the vegetables into a steamer
3. Add enough water and cook on high until vegetables are steamed
4. When ready remove from the steamer and serve

GUACAMOLE

Serves: **2**

Prep Time: **5**   Minutes

Cook Time: **5**   Minutes

Total Time: **10** Minutes

INGREDIENTS

- 1 avocado
- 1 lime juice
- 1 handful of coriander
- 1 tsp olive oil
- 1 tsp salt
- 1 tsp pepper

DIRECTIONS

1. Place all the ingredients in a blender
2. Blend until smooth and transfer to a bowl

Serves: **4-6**

Prep Time: **15**   Minutes

Cook Time: **35**   Minutes

Total Time: **50**   Minutes

INGREDIENTS

- 2 chicken breasts
- Tortilla chips
- Fajita seasoning
- ¼ cup cheddar cheese
- 4-5 mushrooms
- Guacamole
- ¼ cup peppers

DIRECTIONS

1. In a pan heat olive oil and add chopped onion, sauté until soft
2. Add chicken, fajita seasoning and remaining vegetables
3. Cook on low heat for 10-12 minutes
4. Place tortilla chips into a baking dish, sprinkle cheese and bake in the oven until cheese has melted
5. Remove from the oven pour sautéed vegetables and chicken over and tortilla chips and serve

SCRAMBLED EGGS WITH SALMON

Serves: **2**
Prep Time: **10**   Minutes

Cook Time: **20**   Minutes

Total Time: **30**   Minutes

INGREDIENTS

- ½ lb. smoked salmon
- 2 eggs
- 1 avocado
- 1 tsp salt
- 1 tsp pepper
- 1 tps olive oil

DIRECTIONS

1. In a bowl whisk the eggs with salt and pepper
2. In a skillet heat olive oil and pour the egg mixture
3. Add salmon pieces to the mixture and cook for 2-3 minutes per side
4. When ready remove from the skillet, add avocado and serve

CHICKEN WITH RICE

Serves: *4*

Prep Time: *10*   Minutes

Cook Time: *25*   Minutes

Total Time: *35*   Minutes

INGREDIENTS

- 2 chicken breasts
- 1 cup cooked white rice
- 2 tablespoons mayonnaise
- 1 tablespoon curry powder
- 1 zucchini
- 1 cup broccoli
- 1 tablespoon olive oil

DIRECTIONS

1. Cut chicken breast into small pieces and set aside
2. In a pan heat olive oil and cook the chicken breast for 4-5 minutes
3. In another bowl combine mayonnaise, curry powder and add mixture to the chicken
4. Add remaining ingredients and cook for another 10-12 minutes or until the chicken is ready
5. When ready remove from the pot and serve with white rice

ROASTED VEGETABLES

Serves: *2*

Prep Time: *10*   Minutes

Cook Time: *50*   Minutes

Total Time: *60*   Minutes

INGREDIENTS

- 1 carrot
- 2 sweet potatoes
- 1 butternut squash
- 2 parsnips
- 1 rosemary spring
- 2 bay leaves

DIRECTIONS

1. Chop the vegetables into thin slices
2. Place everything in a prepare baking dish
3. Bake at 350 F for 40-45 minutes or until vegetables are golden brown
4. When ready remove from the oven and serve

SAUSAGE PIZZA

Serves: *6-8*

Prep Time: *10*   Minutes

Cook Time: *15*   Minutes

Total Time: 25   Minutes

INGREDIENTS

- 2 pork sausages
- 1 tablespoon olive oil
- 2 garlic cloves
- 1 tsp fennel seeds
- ½ lb. ricotta
- 1 cup mozzarella cheese
- 1 oz. parmesan cheese
- 1 pizza crust

DIRECTIONS

1. Spread tomato sauce on the pizza crust
2. Place all the toppings on the pizza crust
3. Bake the pizza at 425 F for 12-15 minutes
4. When ready remove pizza from the oven and serve

Serves: **6-8**
Prep Time: **10**   Minutes

Cook Time: **15**   Minutes

Total Time: **25**   Minutes

INGREDIENTS

- 1 pizza crust
- 1 tablespoon olive oil
- 1 garlic clove
- 1 cup tomatoes
- 1 cup mozzarella cheese
- 1 carrot
- 1 cucumber

DIRECTIONS

1. Spread tomato sauce on the pizza crust
2. Place all the toppings on the pizza crust
3. Bake the pizza at 425 F for 12-15 minutes
4. When ready remove pizza from the oven and serve

SLAW

Serves: **1**

Prep Time: **5** Minutes

Cook Time: **5** Minutes

Total Time: **10** Minutes

INGREDIENTS

- 1 cabbage
- 1 bunch of baby carrots
- ½ cucumber
- 1 bun of cilantro
- 1 bunch of basil
- 1 onion

DIRECTIONS

1. In a bowl combine all ingredients together and mix well
2. Serve with dressing

EDAMAME FRITATTA

Serves: *2*

Prep Time: *10*   Minutes

Cook Time: *20*   Minutes

Total Time: *30*   Minutes

INGREDIENTS

- 1 cup edamame
- 1 tablespoon olive oil
- ½ red onion
- 2 eggs
- ¼ tsp salt
- 2 oz. cheddar cheese
- 1 garlic clove
- ¼ tsp dill

DIRECTIONS

1. In a bowl whisk eggs with salt and cheese
2. In a frying pan heat olive oil and pour egg mixture
3. Add remaining ingredients and mix well
4. Serve when ready

ONION FRITATTA

Serves: *2*

Prep Time: *10*   Minutes

Cook Time: *20*   Minutes

Total Time: *30*   Minutes

INGREDIENTS

- 1 tablespoon olive oil
- ½ red onion
- 2 eggs
- ¼ tsp salt
- 2 oz. cheddar cheese
- 1 garlic clove
- ¼ tsp dill

DIRECTIONS

1. In a bowl whisk eggs with salt and cheese
2. In a frying pan heat olive oil and pour egg mixture
3. Add remaining ingredients and mix well
4. Serve when ready

LEAF FRITATTA

Serves: *2*

Prep Time: *10*   Minutes

Cook Time: *20*   Minutes

Total Time: *30*   Minutes

INGREDIENTS

- ½ lb. leaf
- 1 tablespoon olive oil
- ½ red onion
- 2 eggs
- ¼ tsp salt
- 2 oz. cheddar cheese
- 1 garlic clove
- ¼ tsp dill

DIRECTIONS

1. In a bowl whisk eggs with salt and cheese
2. In a frying pan heat olive oil and pour egg mixture
3. Add remaining ingredients and mix well
4. Serve when ready

KALE FRITATTA

Serves: *2*

Prep Time: *10* Minutes

Cook Time: *20* Minutes

Total Time: *30* Minutes

INGREDIENTS

- 1 cup kale
- 1 tablespoon olive oil
- ½ red onion
- 2 eggs
- ¼ tsp salt
- 2 oz. cheddar cheese
- 1 garlic clove
- ¼ tsp dill

DIRECTIONS

1. In a skillet sauté kale until tender
2. In a bowl whisk eggs with salt and cheese
3. In a frying pan heat olive oil and pour egg mixture
4. Add remaining ingredients and mix well
5. When ready serve with sautéed kale

JICAMA FRITATTA

Serves: **2**

Prep Time: **10** Minutes

Cook Time: **20** Minutes

Total Time: **30** Minutes

INGREDIENTS

- ½ cup jicama
- 1 tablespoon olive oil
- ½ red onion
- 2 eggs
- ¼ tsp salt
- 2 oz. parmesan cheese
- 1 garlic clove
- ¼ tsp dill

DIRECTIONS

1. In a bowl whisk eggs with salt and parmesan cheese
2. In a frying pan heat olive oil and pour egg mixture
3. Add remaining ingredients and mix well
4. Serve when ready

BROCCOLI FRITATTA

Serves: **2**

Prep Time: **10** Minutes

Cook Time: **20** Minutes

Total Time: **30** Minutes

INGREDIENTS

- 1 cup broccoli
- 1 tablespoon olive oil
- ½ red onion
- 2 eggs
- ¼ tsp salt
- 2 oz. cheddar cheese
- 1 garlic clove
- ¼ tsp dill

DIRECTIONS

1. In a skillet sauté broccoli until tender
2. In a bowl whisk eggs with salt and cheese
3. In a frying pan heat olive oil and pour egg mixture
4. Add remaining ingredients and mix well
5. When ready serve with sautéed broccoli

CAULIFLOWER SANDWICH

Serves: *2*

Prep Time: *10*   Minutes

Cook Time: *30*   Minutes

Total Time: *40*   Minutes

INGREDIENTS

- 1 head cauliflower
- 4 tablespoons olive oil
- ¼ tsp salt
- ½ red onion
- 2 tablespoons tahini
- 1 clove garlic
- 4 slices gluten-free bread
- 1 avocado

DIRECTIONS

1. Toss the cauliflower with olive oil and roast at 400 F for 22-25 minutes
2. In a saucepan sauté the onion until soft
3. Add roasted cauliflower, tahini, olive oil, salt and cook for 1-2 minutes
4. Place everything in a blender and blend until smooth
5. Spread mixture over bread slices

AVOCADO BOATS

Serves: **2**

Prep Time: **10**   Minutes

Cook Time: **10**   Minutes

Total Time: **20**   Minutes

INGREDIENTS

- 1 can chickpeas
- ¼ red onion
- ¼ tsp turmeric
- 1 tablespoon dill
- ½ tsp garlic powder
- 1 tablespoon mustard
- ½ cup tahini
- 2 avocados

DIRECTIONS

1. Cut avocado in half and scoop out part of the interior
2. In a bowl combine together chickpeas with onion, turmeric, dill, garlic, tahini and mustard
3. Mix well and spoon mixture into avocado halves
4. Serve when ready

MEXICAN CORN DIP

Serves: *2*

Prep Time: *10*   Minutes

Cook Time: *20*   Minutes

Total Time: *30*   Minutes

INGREDIENTS

- 2 cups kernels
- 1 tablespoon butter
- 1 jalapeno pepper
- 1 tsp chili powder
- 1 red onion
- ½ cup mayonnaise
- 1 tablespoon lime juice
- 2 tablespoons cilantro

DIRECTIONS

1. In a skillet melt butter over medium heat
2. Add corn and cook for 5-6 minutes
3. Add chili powder, jalapeno, red onion and cook on low heat
4. Add lime juice, mayonnaise and cook for another 2-3 minutes
5. Remove from heat, stir in cilantro and serve with tortilla chips

LEEK QUICHE

Serves: **4**

Prep Time: **10**   Minutes

Cook Time: **50**   Minutes

Total Time: **60**   Minutes

INGREDIENTS

- 1 tablespoon butter
- 1 bunch asparagus
- 1 leek
- ¼ tsp salt
- 2 eggs
- ½ cup vanilla yogurt
- 1 cup almond milk
- 1 cup cheese
- 1 pie crust

DIRECTIONS

1. In a saucepan melt butter, add leek, asparagus, pepper, salt and cook until vegetables are soft
2. In a bowl combine eggs, milk, yogurt and mix well
3. Place egg mixture on the pie crust
4. Top with asparagus and leek
5. Bake at 375 F for 40-45 minutes

6. When ready remove from the oven and serve

ROASTED SQUASH

Serves: **3-4**

Prep Time: **10** Minutes

Cook Time: **20** Minutes

Total Time: **30** Minutes

INGREDIENTS

- 2 delicata squashes
- 2 tablespoons olive oil
- 1 tsp curry powder
- 1 tsp salt

DIRECTIONS

1. Preheat the oven to 400 F
2. Cut everything in half lengthwise
3. Toss everything with olive oil and place onto a prepared baking sheet
4. Roast for 18-20 minutes at 400 F or until golden brown
5. When ready remove from the oven and serve

BRUSSELS SPROUT CHIPS

Serves: **2**

Prep Time: **10** Minutes

Cook Time: **20** Minutes

Total Time: **30** Minutes

INGREDIENTS

- 1 lb. brussels sprouts
- 1 tablespoon olive oil
- 1 tablespoon parmesan cheese
- 1 tsp garlic powder
- 1 tsp seasoning

DIRECTIONS

1. Preheat the oven to 425 F
2. In a bowl toss everything with olive oil and seasoning
3. Spread everything onto a prepared baking sheet
4. Bake for 8-10 minutes or until crisp
5. When ready remove from the oven and serve

CUCUMBER CHIPS

Serves: 2

Prep Time: *10*   Minutes

Cook Time: *20*   Minutes

Total Time: *30*   Minutes

INGREDIENTS

- 1 lb. cucumber
- 1 tsp salt
- 1 tsp smoked paprika
- 1 tablespoon olive oil

DIRECTIONS

1. Preheat the oven to 425 F
2. In a bowl toss everything with olive oil and seasoning
3. Spread everything onto a prepared baking sheet
4. Bake for 8-10 minutes or until crisp
5. When ready remove from the oven and serve

SQUASH CHIPS

Serves: *2*
Prep Time: *10*   Minutes

Cook Time: *20*   Minutes

Total Time: *30*   Minutes

INGREDIENTS

- 1 lb. squash
- 1 tsp salt
- 1 tsp smoked paprika
- 1 tablespoon olive oil

DIRECTIONS

1. Preheat the oven to 425 F
2. In a bowl toss everything with olive oil and seasoning
3. Spread everything onto a prepared baking sheet
4. Bake for 8-10 minutes or until crisp
5. When ready remove from the oven and serve

PASTA

SIMPLE SPAGHETTI

Serves: 2
Prep Time: 5   Minutes

Cook Time: 15   Minutes

Total Time: 20   Minutes

INGREDIENTS

- 10 oz. spaghetti
- 2 eggs
- ½ cup parmesan cheese
- 1 tsp black pepper
- Olive oil
- 1 tsp parsley
- 2 cloves garlic

DIRECTIONS

1. In a pot boil spaghetti (or any other type of pasta), drain and set aside
2. In a bowl whish eggs with parmesan cheese
3. In a skillet heat olive oil, add garlic and cook for 1-2 minutes
4. Pour egg mixture and mix well
5. Add pasta and stir well

6. When ready garnish with parsley and serve

Serves: *2*

Prep Time: *5*   Minutes

Cook Time: *15*   Minutes

Total Time: *20*   Minutes

INGREDIENTS

- ¼ cup mayonnaise
- ¼ cup sweet chili sauce
- 1 tablespoon lime juice
- 1 garlic clove
- 8 z. pasta
- 1 lb. shrimp
- ¼ tsp paprika

DIRECTIONS

1. In a pot boil spaghetti (or any other type of pasta), drain and set aside
2. Place all the ingredients for the sauce in a pot and bring to a simmer
3. Add pasta and mix well
4. When ready garnish with parmesan cheese and serve

PASTA WITH OLIVES AND TOMATOES

Serves: 2
Prep Time: 5   Minutes

Cook Time: 15   Minutes

Total Time: 20   Minutes

INGREDIENTS

- 8 oz. pasta
- 3 tablespoons olive oil
- 2 cloves garlic
- 5-6 anchovy fillets
- 2 cups tomatoes
- 1 cup olives
- ½ cup basil leaves

DIRECTIONS

1. In a pot boil spaghetti (or any other type of pasta), drain and set aside
2. Place all the ingredients for the sauce in a pot and bring to a simmer
3. Add pasta and mix well
4. When ready garnish with parmesan cheese and serve

SALAD

MORNING SALAD

Serves: **2**

Prep Time: **5**   Minutes

Cook Time: **5**   Minutes

Total Time: **10**   Minutes

INGREDIENTS

- 1 onion
- 1 tsp cumin
- 1 tablespoon olive oil
- 1 avocado
- ¼ lb. cooked lentils
- 1 oz. walnuts
- Coriander
- ¼ lb. feta cheese
- Salad dressing of choice
- 8-10 baby carrots

DIRECTIONS

1. In a bowl combine all ingredients together and mix well
2. Add dressing and serve

TOMATO SOUP

Serves: *1*
Prep Time: 5   Minutes

Cook Time: *10*   Minutes

Total Time: *15*   Minutes

INGREDIENTS

- ¾ cup chicken broth
- 2 tbs tomato paste
- 2 tbs milk
- ½ cup tomatoes
- 1 tbs vinegar
- 1 tbs onion
- 1 clove garlic
- 1 tsp oregano
- Salt
- Pepper
- Basil leaves

DIRECTIONS

1. Pulse the ingredients in a food processor, saving the basil for garnish.
2. Cook the mixture until heated.
3. Serve garnished with basil leaves and toast.

CRAB SALAD

Serves: *1*

Prep Time: *5* Minutes

Cook Time: *10* Minutes

Total Time: *15* Minutes

INGREDIENTS

- ½ cup celery
- 1 tbs vinegar
- 1 tsp seasoning
- 100 g crab
- Red pepper flakes
- 2 tbs lemon juice
- 2 tbs onion

DIRECTIONS

1. Sauté the ingredients in a pan until celery is tender.
2. Season to taste.
3. Serve when ready

ASIAN SALAD

Serves: **1**

Prep Time: **5** Minutes

Cook Time: **5** Minutes

Total Time: **10** Minutes

INGREDIENTS

- ½ cup orange segments
- 1 packet stevia
- 1 toast
- 100g chicken breast
- ¼ tsp salt
- Orange citrus dressing
- 2 cups romaine lettuce

DIRECTIONS

1. Cook the chicken in a skillet until golden.
2. Combine all of the ingredients in a bowl.
3. Serve immediately.

CHICKEN SALAD

Serves: *1*

Prep Time: *5*   Minutes

Cook Time: *10*   Minutes

Total Time: *15*   Minutes

INGREDIENTS

- 100g chicken
- ½ tsp onion powder
- ½ tsp garlic powder
- ½ tsp oregano
- 1 tsp paprika
- ½ tsp thyme
- ½ tsp black pepper
- ¼ tsp salad greens

DIRECTIONS

1. Rub the chicken with the combined spices.
2. Grill the pink until golden.
3. Serve over the salad greens and desired dressing.

CUCUMBER SALAD

Serves: *1*

Prep Time: 5   Minutes

Cook Time: *0*   Minutes

Total Time: 5   Minutes

INGREDIENTS

- ¼ tsp salt
- 2 tsp parsley
- ¼ cup vinegar
- 2 tsp green onion
- Pepper
- Stevia
- 1 cucumber

DIRECTIONS

1. Chop the cucumber.
2. Mix the ingredients in a bowl.
3. Refrigerate for at least 10 minutes, then serve.

GRAPEFRUIT SALAD

Serves: *1*
Prep Time: *10*   Minutes

Cook Time: *0*   Minutes

Total Time: *10*   Minutes

INGREDIENTS

- 2 tbs apple vinegar
- Grapefruit juice
- ½ tsp ginger
- Salt
- 1 red grapefruit
- 1 cucumber
- Pepper
- Cilantro
- 2 tbs onion
- Ruby red dressing

DIRECTIONS

1. Peel the grapefruit and cut it into cubes.
2. Mix with the rest of the ingredients and season.
3. Serve topped with red dressing.

APPLE SALAD

Serves: *2*

Prep Time: *5*   Minutes

Cook Time: *0*   Minutes

Total Time: *5*   Minutes

INGREDIENTS

- ½ cup green apple
- 1 tbs lemon juice
- Salt
- Pepper
- Stevia
- ½ cup cucumber
- 2 tbs apple cider vinegar

DIRECTIONS

1. Chop the apple and cucumber.
2. Combine the ingredients and add stevia.
3. Serve immediately.

COLESLAW

Serves: *1*
Prep Time: *10*   Minutes

Cook Time: *0*   Minutes

Total Time: *10*   Minutes

INGREDIENTS

- 1 ½ cups cabbage
- ¼ tsp onion powder
- Cayenne pepper
- Salt
- Pepper
- 2 tbs vinegar
- 2 tbs lemon juice
- 1 tsp horseradish
- 1 clove garlic
- ½ tsp mustard

DIRECTIONS

1. Slice the cabbage.
2. Mix the rest of the ingredients in a bowl.
3. Pour the mixture over the cabbage and serve.

LOBSTER SALAD

Serves: *1*

Prep Time: 5   Minutes

Cook Time: 5   Minutes

Total Time: *10*   Minutes

INGREDIENTS

- 100g lobster
- 1 serving Tarragon Vinaigrette
- 2 tbs lemon juice
- 1 tbs tarragon
- ½ tsp garlic powder
- 2 tbs onion
- 1 tbs green onion

DIRECTIONS

1. Cook the lobster.
2. Sauté the lobster, lemon juice, green onion, onion, tarragon, garlic powder, salt, and pepper until onion is tender.
3. Top the lettuce with the lobster mixture.
4. Serve topped with Tarragon Vinaigrette.

Serves: *1*
Prep Time: *10*   Minutes

Cook Time: *20*   Minutes

Total Time: *30*   Minutes

INGREDIENTS

- 2 tbs lemon juice
- 1 tbs onion
- 1 tbs parsley
- Salt
- Radishes
- Pepper

DIRECTIONS

1. Combine all of the ingredients in a bowl.
2. Refrigerate for at least 20 minutes.
3. Serve.

SPINACH SALAD

Serves: **1**

Prep Time: **5** Minutes

Cook Time: **5** Minutes

Total Time: **10** Minutes

INGREDIENTS

- 1 bunch spinach
- Pepper
- Mint leaves
- 2 tbs vinegar
- 2 tbs lemon juice
- 5 strawberries
- ¼ tsp Stevia
- Salt

DIRECTIONS

1. Blend 2 strawberries, lemon juice, vinegar, Stevia, salt, and pepper together.
2. Pour the dressing over the salad and the sliced remained strawberry.
3. Serve topped with mint leaves.

THIRD COOKBOOK

CAULIFLOWER SOUP

Serves: *4*

Prep Time: *10* Minutes

Cook Time: *20* Minutes

Total Time: *30* Minutes

INGREDIENTS

- 1 tablespoon olive oil
- 1 lb. cauliflower
- ¼ red onion
- ½ cup all-purpose flour
- ¼ tsp salt
- ¼ tsp pepper
- 1 can vegetable broth
- 1 cup heavy cream

DIRECTIONS

1. In a saucepan heat olive oil and sauté cauliflower until tender
2. Add remaining ingredients to the saucepan and bring to a boil
3. When all the vegetables are tender transfer to a blender and blend until smooth
4. Pour soup into bowls, garnish with parsley and serve

Serves: *4*

Prep Time: *10*   Minutes

Cook Time: *30*   Minutes

Total Time: *40*   Minutes

INGREDIENTS

- 2 tablespoons unsalted butter
- ½ cup minced onion
- ½ cup mushrooms
- 2 tablespoons all-purpose flour
- ¼ cup low sodium chicken broth
- ¼ cup almond milk
- pepper

DIRECTIONS

1. In a soup pot add all soup ingredients
2. Sauté for 5-6 minutes
3. Add water simmer for 20-30 minutes
4. Season with pepper
5. When ready, pour into bowls and serve

ZUCCHINI SOUP

Serves: **4**
Prep Time: **10**   Minutes

Cook Time: **20**   Minutes

Total Time: **30**   Minutes

INGREDIENTS

- 1 tablespoon olive oil
- 1 lb. zucchini
- ¼ red onion
- ½ cup all-purpose flour
- ¼ tsp salt
- ¼ tsp pepper
- 1 can vegetable broth
- 1 cup heavy cream

DIRECTIONS

1. In a saucepan heat olive oil and sauté zucchini until tender
2. Add remaining ingredients to the saucepan and bring to a boil
3. When all the vegetables are tender transfer to a blender and blend until smooth
4. Pour soup into bowls, garnish with parsley and serve

CELERY SOUP

Serves: **4**
Prep Time: **10**   Minutes

Cook Time: **20**   Minutes

Total Time: **30**   Minutes

INGREDIENTS

- 1 tablespoon olive oil
- 1 lb. celery
- ¼ red onion
- ½ cup all-purpose flour
- ¼ tsp salt
- ¼ tsp pepper
- 1 can vegetable broth
- 1 cup heavy cream

DIRECTIONS

1. In a saucepan heat olive oil and sauté celery until tender
2. Add remaining ingredients to the saucepan and bring to a boil
3. When all the vegetables are tender transfer to a blender and blend until smooth
4. Pour soup into bowls, garnish with parsley and serve

CARROT SOUP

Serves: **4**

Prep Time: **10** Minutes

Cook Time: **20** Minutes

Total Time: **30** Minutes

INGREDIENTS

- 1 tablespoon olive oil
- 1 lb. carrots
- ¼ red onion
- ½ cup all-purpose flour
- ¼ tsp salt
- ¼ tsp pepper
- 1 can vegetable broth
- 1 cup heavy cream

DIRECTIONS

1. In a saucepan heat olive oil and sauté carrots until tender
2. Add remaining ingredients to the saucepan and bring to a boil
3. When all the vegetables are tender transfer to a blender and blend until smooth
4. Pour soup into bowls, garnish with parsley and serve

CUCUMBER SOUP

Serves: *4*

Prep Time: *10* Minutes

Cook Time: *20* Minutes

Total Time: *30* Minutes

INGREDIENTS

- 1 tablespoon olive oil
- 1 lb. cucumber
- ¼ red onion
- ½ cup all-purpose flour
- ¼ tsp salt
- ¼ tsp pepper
- 1 can vegetable broth
- 1 cup heavy cream

DIRECTIONS

1. In a saucepan heat olive oil and sauté cucumber until tender
2. Add remaining ingredients to the saucepan and bring to a boil
3. When all the vegetables are tender transfer to a blender and blend until smooth
4. Pour soup into bowls, garnish with parsley and serve

GOAT'S CHEESE RAREBIT

Serves: **4**

Prep Time: **10**   Minutes

Cook Time: **30**   Minutes

Total Time: **40**   Minutes

INGREDIENTS

- 1 oz. olive oil
- 150 ml soya milk
- 6 oz. goat cheese
- 1 oz. flour
- ½ tsp mustard
- pepper
- 1 egg yolk
- 4 bread slices

DIRECTIONS

1. In a saucepan add butter, cheese, soya milk and cook on low heat
2. Stir in flour and bring mixture to a boil
3. Remove from heat add mustard, pepper and whisk in the egg yolks
4. Toast the bread and spread mixture between the slices

5. Place on a grill and cook until golden

SMOKED MACKEREL PATE

Serves: *2*
Prep Time: *10*   Minutes

Cook Time: *10*   Minutes

Total Time: *20*   Minutes

INGREDIENTS

- 7 oz. smoked mackerel fillets
- 2 onions
- 1 lemon
- 3 oz. cream cheese
- 1 tablespoon creamed horseradish
- pepper

DIRECTIONS

1. Cut mackerel into small chunks
2. In a bowl mix cream cheese, mackerel, creamed horseradish, onions and zest of 1 lemon
3. Mix with lemon juice and season with pepper and pate that should be ready

Serves: **4**

Prep Time: **10**   Minutes

Cook Time: **30**   Minutes

Total Time: **40**   Minutes

INGREDIENTS

- 7 oz. basil pesto
- 3 oz. cream cheese
- 3 oz. sour cream
- 2 tablespoons parmesan cheese

DIRECTIONS

1. In a bowl add cream cheese, pesto, sour cream and parmesan cheese
2. Mix well and serve when ready

CAULIFLOWER CHEESE

Serves: **6**

Prep Time: **10**   Minutes

Cook Time: **20**   Minutes

Total Time: **30**   Minutes

INGREDIENTS

- 1 cauliflower
- 500 ml milk
- 3 tablespoons flour
- 2 oz. butter
- 3 oz. cheddar cheese
- 2 tablespoons breadcrumbs

DIRECTIONS

1. Preheat the oven to 400 F
2. In a saucepan add cauliflower and cook for 5-8 minutes
3. Add milk, butter, flour and whisk until mixture boils
4. Stir in cheese and pour over the cauliflower
5. Scatter over the remaining cheese and breadcrumbs
6. Bake cauliflower cheese for 18-20 minutes

Serves: **4**

Prep Time: **10**   Minutes

Cook Time: **30**   Minutes

Total Time: **40**   Minutes

INGREDIENTS

- 2 tablespoons olive oil
- 1 onion
- 500 ml chicken stock
- 10 sage leaves
- 6 oz. Arborio rice
- 9 oz. pumpkin
- 2 oz. butter
- 1 pinch black pepper
- parmesan cheese

DIRECTIONS

1. In a saucepan add ½ chicken stock and cook on low heat, add sage, onion, rice and continue to simmer
2. Add pumpkin, remaining stock and cook until stock is absorbed and pumpkin is soft
3. Stir in butter, season with pepper and divide into 2-3 servings
4. Add grated cheese and serve

GREEN PESTO PASTA

Serves: **2**

Prep Time: **5** Minutes

Cook Time: **15** Minutes

Total Time: **20** Minutes

INGREDIENTS

- 4 oz. spaghetti
- 2 cups basil leaves
- 2 garlic cloves
- ¼ cup olive oil
- 2 tablespoons parmesan cheese
- ½ tsp black pepper

DIRECTIONS

5. Bring water to a boil and add pasta
6. In a blend add parmesan cheese, basil leaves, garlic and blend
7. Add olive oil, pepper and blend again
8. Pour pesto onto pasta and serve when ready

Serves: **4**

Prep Time: **10** Minutes

Cook Time: **20** Minutes

Total Time: **30** Minutes

INGREDIENTS

- 1 lb. beef
- 1 garlic clove
- 1 chili
- 1 onion
- 1 oz. fresh basil
- 1 tablespoon soy sauce
- 1 tablespoon vegetable oil

DIRECTIONS

1. Fry garlic, chili and mince over medium heat
2. Add the rest of ingredients and cook for 18-20 minutes
3. Remove from heat and serve with rice

PORK CHOPS

Serves: **4**

Prep Time: **10** Minutes

Cook Time: **30** Minutes

Total Time: **40** Minutes

INGREDIENTS

- 2 pork chops
- 1 tsp mustard
- 1 tsp oil
- 1 spring onion
- 1 clove garlic
- 1 tablespoon breadcrumbs
- 1 pinch dried hers

DIRECTIONS

1. Preheat the oven to 375 F
2. Spread the mustard over the pork chop
3. In a bowl add garlic, dried herbs, breadcrumbs, onions and mix well
4. Spread the herb mixture on top of each pork chop
5. Bake for 20-25 minutes
6. Remove and serve with boiled potatoes

BEEF BURGERS

Serves: **4**

Prep Time: **10**   Minutes

Cook Time: **20**   Minutes

Total Time: **30**   Minutes

INGREDIENTS

- 1 lb. minced beef
- 1 onion
- 1 pinch dried herb
- 1 pinch black pepper

DIRECTIONS

1. Preheat the grill to hot
2. In a bowl mix all ingredients together
3. Divide mixture into 4 portion and shape into patties
4. Grill for 5-6 minutes per side or until brown
5. Serve in a burger bun with potato fries

BAKED FISH

Serves: **4**

Prep Time: **10**   Minutes

Cook Time: **30**   Minutes

Total Time: **40**   Minutes

INGREDIENTS

- 1 lb. boneless fish fillets
- juice of 1 lemon
- 1 tablespoon unsalted butter
- 1 pinch rosemary

DIRECTIONS

1. Preheat the oven to 325 F
2. Place the fish in a shallow baking dish
3. In a bowl mix all remaining ingredients
4. Dot over fish fillets
5. Bake for 25 minutes or until fish is tender
6. Serve with vegetables

MINT COUSCOUS

Serves: *4*
Prep Time: *10*   Minutes

Cook Time: *15*   Minutes

Total Time: *25*   Minutes

INGREDIENTS

- ½ lb. couscous
- 500 ml water
- 2 tablespoons mint
- 2 teaspoons olive oil

DIRECTIONS

1. In a saucepan bring water to a boil
2. Add couscous and cover with a lid
3. Drizzle oil, mint and cook until soft
4. Season with black pepper and serve with baked fish

FRESH PORK PATTIES

Serves:	*8*	
Prep Time:	*10*	minutes
Cook Time:	*20*	minutes
Total Time:	*30*	minutes

INGREDIENTS

- 2 lbs fresh lean ground pork
- ½ teaspoon black pepper
- 1 teaspoon lemon juice
- ½ teaspoon ground sage
- ½ teaspoon marjoram
- 1 teaspoon paprika

DIRECTIONS

1. Combine all ingredients in a bowl and mix them
2. Add 2-3 tablespoons water to the pork mixture and mix
3. Form into 8 patties
4. Spray skillet with cooking spray
5. Sprinkle the patties with paprika
6. Cook until crispy brown
7. Remove excess fat
8. Cooked pork patties can be frozen for later if you want

POTATO SALAD

Serves: **2**

Prep Time: **5** Minutes

Cook Time: **5** Minutes

Total Time: **10** Minutes

INGREDIENTS

- 2 lb. cooked red potatoes
- 1 tablespoon salt
- ¼ cup olive oil
- ¼ cup parsley
- ¼ cup green onions
- 1 tablespoon lemon juice
- 1 tsp mustard
- 2 stalks celery

DIRECTIONS

1. In a bowl mix all ingredients and mix well
2. Serve with dressing

Serves: **2**

Prep Time: **5**   Minutes

Cook Time: **5**   Minutes

Total Time: **10**   Minutes

INGREDIENTS

- 1 can black beans
- 1 can chickpeas
- 1 red onion
- 2 stalks celery
- 1 cucumber
- ½ cup parsley
- 1 tablespoon mint
- 2 cloves garlic

DIRECTIONS

1. In a bowl combine all ingredients together and mix well
2. Serve with dressing

Serves: **2**

Prep Time: **5**   Minutes

Cook Time: **5**   Minutes

Total Time: **10**   Minutes

INGREDIENTS

- 1 bunch kale
- 1 apple
- 1 fennel
- 4 oz. feta cheese
- ½ cup cranberries
- 1 cup maple syrup salad dressing

DIRECTIONS

1. In a bowl combine all ingredients together and mix well
2. Serve with dressing

TOMATO & SPINACH SALAD

Serves: 2

Prep Time: 5   Minutes

Cook Time: 5   Minutes

Total Time: *10*   Minutes

INGREDIENTS

- 1 cup quinoa
- 1 cup tomatoes
- 1 cup baby spinach
- 1 tablespoon olive oil
- 1 cup lemon salad dressing

DIRECTIONS

1. In a bowl combine all ingredients together and mix well
2. Serve with dressing

Serves: **2**

Prep Time: **5**   Minutes

Cook Time: **5**   Minutes

Total Time: **10**   Minutes

INGREDIENTS

- 1 cup cooked wild rice
- 1 tsp olive oil
- 6 oz. arugula
- ¼ cup basil
- ½ cup cranberries
- ½ cup goat cheese
- 1 cup lemon salad dressing

DIRECTIONS

1. In a bowl combine all ingredients together and mix well
2. Serve with dressing

KALE SALAD

Serves: **2**

Prep Time: **5**   Minutes

Cook Time: **5**   Minutes

Total Time: **10** Minutes

INGREDIENTS

- 1 bunch kale
- 1 cup cooked grains
- 2 carrots
- 1 radish
- 1 tablespoon pepitas
- 1 cup tahini dressing

DIRECTIONS

1. In a bowl combine all ingredients together and mix well
2. Serve with dressing

Serves: *2*
Prep Time: *5*   Minutes

Cook Time: *5*   Minutes

Total Time: *10*   Minutes

INGREDIENTS

- 1 head leaf lettuce
- 1 red bell pepper
- 2 mangoes
- 1 cup green onion
- ½ cup peanuts
- ½ cup cilantro
- 1 cup peanut dressing

DIRECTIONS

1. In a bowl combine all ingredients together and mix well
2. Serve with dressing

HERBED SALAD

Serves: **2**

Prep Time: **5**   Minutes

Cook Time: **5**   Minutes

Total Time: **10** Minutes

INGREDIENTS

- 2 lb. cooked white potatoes
- 2 tablespoons olive oil
- ½ cup parsley
- ½ cup green onion
- 1 tablespoon lemon juice
- 1 tsp mustard
- 2 cloves garlic
- 1 tsp black pepper
- 1 tsp oregano

DIRECTIONS

1. In a bowl combine all ingredients together and mix well
2. Serve with dressing

BEET SALAD

Serves: **2**
Prep Time: **5**   Minutes

Cook Time: **5**   Minutes

Total Time: **10**   Minutes

INGREDIENTS

- 1 cup cooked quinoa
- 1 cup edamame
- 1 cup pepitas
- 1 beet
- 1 carrot
- 1 cup baby spinach
- 1 avocado
- 1 cup lemon salad dressing

DIRECTIONS

1. In a bowl combine all ingredients together and mix well
2. Serve with dressing

Serves: *2*
Prep Time: *5*   Minutes

Cook Time: *5*   Minutes

Total Time: *10* Minutes

INGREDIENTS

- 6 oz. greens
- 1 apple
- 1 cup cranberries
- ½ cup pepitas
- 3 oz. feta cheese

DIRECTIONS

1. In a bowl combine all ingredients together and mix well
2. Serve with dressing

Serves: *1*
Prep Time: *5*   Minutes

Cook Time: *10*   Minutes

Total Time: *15*   Minutes

INGREDIENTS

- 3 oz. shrimp
- ¼ cup zucchini
- ½ cup fiesta garden salsa
- ¼ oz. cheese
- cilantro
- 1 tortilla

DIRECTIONS

1. In a bowl add zucchini, shrimp and pour salsa over
2. Microwave for 4-5 minutes and sprinkle with grated cheese and cilantro
3. Microwave tortilla for 10-20 seconds and serve with shrimp

CAULIFLOWER FRITTERS

Serves: *8*
Prep Time: *10*   Minutes

Cook Time: *30*   Minutes

Total Time: *40*   Minutes

INGREDIENTS

- 1 head of cauliflower
- ¼ tsp chili powder
- 2 cloves garlic
- 2 tablespoons cilantro
- 1 tsp salt
- ¼ tsp black pepper
- 2 eggs
- 3 tablespoons cornmeal
- ½ cup flour
- 4 tablespoons nutritional yeast

DIRECTIONS

1. Cook cauliflower florets by steaming for 5-6 minutes
2. Mix the cauliflower with chili powder, cilantro, garlic, pepper and salt
3. In another bowl beat the egg, add cauliflower mixture, flour, cornmeal, and yeast

4. Add ¼ cup of the mixture to the pan and press down the fritter
5. Cook until golden brown for 3-4 minutes per side
6. When ready, remove and serve

FRENCH TOAST SANDWICHES

Serves: *2*

Prep Time: *5*   Minutes

Cook Time: *10*   Minutes

Total Time: *15*   Minutes

INGREDIENTS

- 4 thin slices bread
- 2 eggs
- 1/3 cup almond milk
- ¼ tsp vanilla extract
- 1 tablespoon cream cheese
- 1 tablespoon apricot preserves
- ½ cup maple syrup

DIRECTIONS

1. In a bowl combine vanilla extract, eggs, almond milk, and mix well
2. Make 2 sandwiches with cream cheese and preserve
3. Place sandwiches in egg mixture on both sides
4. In a skillet cook sandwiches for 2-3 minutes per side or until golden brown
5. When ready remove and serve

Serves: **6**

Prep Time: **10**   Minutes

Cook Time: **90**   Minutes

Total Time: **100**   Minutes

INGREDIENTS

- ½ cup olive oil
- 1 eggplant
- 1 onion
- 2 garlic cloves
- 1 lb. potatoes
- 5 tomatoes
- 10 cherry tomatoes
- 1 cup tomato passata
- 1 cup water
- 1 tablespoon dried oregano
- 1 tablespoon parsley
- 1 tsp salt

DIRECTIONS

1. Preheat the oven to 400 F
2. In a frying pan add olive oil, eggplant and cook for 6-7 minutes

3. Add garlic, onion and sauté for 5-6 minutes

4. Add potato, zucchini, passata, tomatoes, and water

5. Sprinkle with oregano, parsley, pepper, and salt

6. Mix well and transfer to a baking dish, drizzle with olive oil and bake for 45-55 minutes or until the top has browned

7. When ready remove and serve

GRILLED SALMON STEAKS

Serves: *4*
Prep Time: *5*   Minutes

Cook Time: *15* Minutes

Total Time: *20* Minutes

INGREDIENTS

- 2 salmon steaks
- 2 tablespoons dipping sauce
- 1 tsp cooking oil

DIRECTIONS

1. Heat grill and rub with cooking oil
2. Baste steaks with sauce
3. Cook for 4-5 minutes per side
4. Don't overcook
5. When ready remove and serve

ORIENTAL GREENS

Serves: *8*
Prep Time: *10*   Minutes

Cook Time: *90*   Minutes

Total Time: *100* Minutes

INGREDIENTS

- ¼ cup green beans
- ¼ cup snow peas
- 1 cup cauliflower florets
- 1 cup water chestnuts
- 2 radishes
- 2 scallions
- ½ cup red onion
- 1 tsp powdered ginger
- ½ cup rice wine vinegar

DIRECTIONS

1. In a bowl combine cauliflower floret, radish slices, onions, water chestnuts and mix well
2. In another bowl combine rice wine vinegar, powdered ginger and pour over vegetables
3. Refrigerate for 1-2 hours
4. When ready remove and serve

BROCCOLI CASSEROLE

Serves: **4**

Prep Time: **10**   Minutes

Cook Time: **15**   Minutes

Total Time: **25**   Minutes

INGREDIENTS

- 1 onion
- 2 chicken breasts
- 2 tablespoons unsalted butter
- 2 eggs
- 2 cups cooked rice
- 2 cups cheese
- 1 cup parmesan cheese
- 2 cups cooked broccoli

DIRECTIONS

1. Sauté the veggies and set aside
2. Preheat the oven to 425 F
3. Transfer the sautéed veggies to a baking dish, add remaining ingredients to the baking dish
4. Mix well, add seasoning and place the dish in the oven
5. Bake for 12-15 minutes or until slightly brown
6. When ready remove from the oven and serve

BEAN FRITATTA

Serves: **2**
Prep Time: **10** Minutes

Cook Time: **20** Minutes

Total Time: **30** Minutes

INGREDIENTS

- 1 cup black beans
- 1 tablespoon olive oil
- ½ red onion
- 2 eggs
- ¼ tsp salt
- 2 oz. cheddar cheese
- 1 garlic clove
- ¼ tsp dill

DIRECTIONS

1. In a bowl whisk eggs with salt and cheese
2. In a frying pan heat olive oil and pour egg mixture
3. Add remaining ingredients and mix well
4. Serve when ready

ROASTED SQUASH

Serves: **3-4**
Prep Time: **10** Minutes

Cook Time: **20** Minutes

Total Time: **30** Minutes

INGREDIENTS

- 2 delicata squashes
- 2 tablespoons olive oil
- 1 tsp curry powder
- 1 tsp salt

DIRECTIONS

1. Preheat the oven to 400 F
2. Cut everything in half lengthwise
3. Toss everything with olive oil and place onto a prepared baking sheet
4. Roast for 18-20 minutes at 400 F or until golden brown
5. When ready remove from the oven and serve

POTATO CHIPS

Serves: **2**

Prep Time: **10** Minutes

Cook Time: **20** Minutes

Total Time: **30** Minutes

INGREDIENTS

- 1 lb. potatoes
- 1 tsp salt
- 1 tsp paprika
- 1 tablespoon olive oil

DIRECTIONS

1. Preheat the oven to 425 F
2. In a bowl toss everything with olive oil and seasoning
3. Spread everything onto a prepared baking sheet
4. Bake for 8-10 minutes or until crisp
5. When ready remove from the oven and serve

PIZZA

ZUCCHINI PIZZA

Serves: **6-8**

Prep Time: **10**   Minutes

Cook Time: **15**   Minutes

Total Time: **25**   Minutes

INGREDIENTS

- 1 pizza crust
- ½ cup tomato sauce
- ¼ black pepper
- 1 cup zucchini slices
- 1 cup mozzarella cheese
- 1 cup olives

DIRECTIONS

1. Spread tomato sauce on the pizza crust
2. Place all the toppings on the pizza crust
3. Bake the pizza at 425 F for 12-15 minutes
4. When ready remove pizza from the oven and serve

TUSCAN PIZZA

Serves:	*6-8*
Prep Time:	*10* Minutes
Cook Time:	*15* Minutes
Total Time:	*25* Minutes

INGREDIENTS

- 1 pizza crust
- 200 g prosciutto
- Basil leaves
- 1 cup tomato sauce
- 1 cup mozzarella
- 1 cup tomato slices

DIRECTIONS

1. Spread tomato sauce on the pizza crust
2. Place all the toppings on the pizza crust
3. Bake the pizza at 425 F for 12-15 minutes
4. When ready remove pizza from the oven and serve

MARGHERITA PIZZA

Serves: **6-8**

Prep Time: **10** Minutes

Cook Time: **15** Minutes

Total Time: **25** Minutes

INGREDIENTS

- 1 pizza crust
- 1 cup tomato sauce
- 1 tablespoon olive oil
- 1 cup mozzarella

DIRECTIONS

1. Spread tomato sauce on the pizza crust
2. Place all the toppings on the pizza crust
3. Bake the pizza at 425 F for 12-15 minutes
4. When ready remove pizza from the oven and serve

SHAKSHUKA PIZZA

Serves: **6-8**

Prep Time: **10**   Minutes

Cook Time: **15**   Minutes

Total Time: **25**   Minutes

INGREDIENTS

- 1 pizza crust
- 1 cup marinara sauce
- 1 tsp parprika
- 1 red onion
- 1 cup roasted red peppers
- 1 cup crumbled feta cheese
- 1 cup arugula
- 1 cup mozzarella

DIRECTIONS

1. Spread tomato sauce on the pizza crust
2. Place all the toppings on the pizza crust
3. Bake the pizza at 425 F for 12-15 minutes
4. When ready remove pizza from the oven and serve

THANK YOU FOR READING THIS BOOK!